I scream,
you scream,
we all scream
for ice cream!

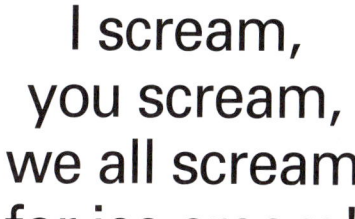

But do you know how
ice cream is made?

Ice cream starts on a dairy farm.

Twice a day farmers milk their cows— by hand

or by machine.

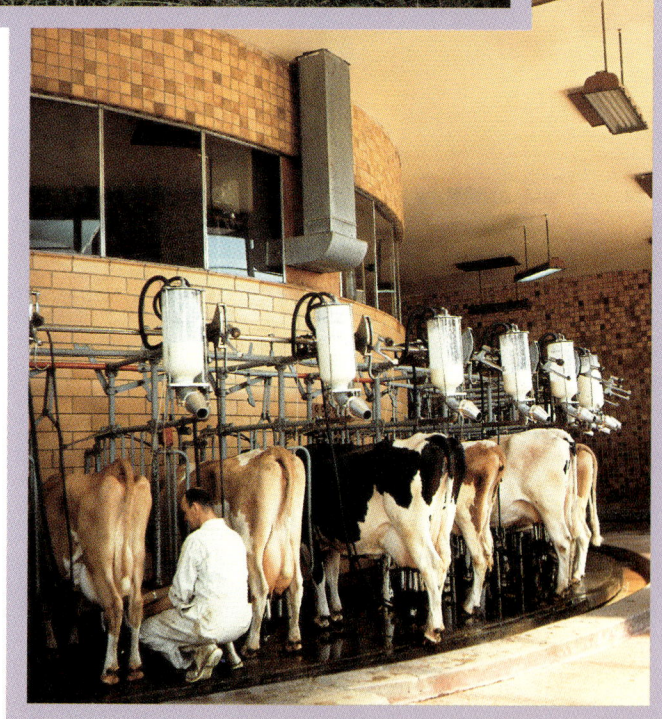

A truck picks up the milk

and brings it to an ice cream factory.

The factory has lots of special machines.

Pumps and pipes move the milk from one machine to the other.

First the workers take the cream out of the milk.

Then they put together just the right amount of milk, cream, and sugar.

That's called "making the mix."

They heat the mix to kill the germs.

That's called "pasteurization."

They squeeze the mix through tiny holes to blend everything together.

That's called "homogenization."

Then they add the flavors. Here goes some strawberry syrup!

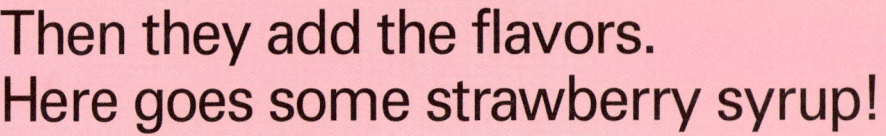

A big freezer stirs and chills the mix.

Machines drop fruit, nuts, or chocolate chips into some of the flavors.

The mix is now yummy, soft ice cream. The ice cream makers taste it to make sure it's good. That's part of their job!

The ice cream is ready to be packed.

Here it comes!

The soft ice cream becomes firm in a very cold room.

Refrigerated trucks take the ice cream to the stores.

Now eat it quickly before it melts!